I0841968

The Power of Evidence: Decoding Facts and Authorities

BARAK ARWELL

Copyright © 2023 by Barak Arwell
All rights reserved. This book or any portion thereof
may not be reproduced or used in any manner whatsoever
without the express written permission of the publisher
except for the use of brief quotations in a
book review.

INTRODUCTION

In an era defined by a relentless surge of information and an increasingly interconnected world, the concepts of facts and authorities have taken on a profound significance. The very foundations of knowledge, belief, and decision-making are shaped by these twin pillars, guiding us through the labyrinthine corridors of human understanding. Welcome to a journey that delves into the intricate tapestry of reality, where we uncover the undeniable power that evidence and expertise hold in shaping our perceptions, decisions, and the course of society itself. This is "The Power of Evidence: Decoding Facts and Authorities."

At its core, this book is a clarion call to the curious and the discerning, an exploration of how we come to know what we know, and a tribute to the relentless pursuit of truth that defines the human experience. In the pages that follow, we will unravel the nuances of facts and authorities, unveiling the symbiotic relationship that underpins our grasp of reality.

Facts, often held as irrefutable truths, serve as the building blocks of knowledge. From the simplest observations to the most complex scientific theories, facts are the bedrock upon which our understanding of the world is constructed. They provide a common ground for discourse, a shared language that transcends the boundaries of culture, language, and ideology. But, as we shall see, the nature of facts is far from simplistic; their interpretation and application are influenced by a myriad of factors, including cultural context, cognitive biases, and the ever-evolving landscape of human discovery.

Enter authorities – the voices of expertise and experience that guide us through the intricate labyrinth of knowledge. These individuals and institutions, recognized for their wisdom, skills, and contributions, serve as beacons in the sea of information. They curate, validate, and disseminate facts, acting as gatekeepers to the realms of truth. However, the age-old adage, "Trust, but verify," reminds us that even the most revered authorities are subject to scrutiny. The dynamics between the quest for factual accuracy and the role of authorities in shaping our beliefs form a critical undercurrent in our exploration.

As we navigate this terrain, we will encounter the shifting landscapes of truth and deception, information and misinformation. We will delve into case studies that illuminate the profound impact of both accurate and distorted information, exploring historical moments where the balance between facts and authorities has shaped the course of events. From the scientific revolution to contemporary debates on climate change, artificial intelligence, and social justice, we will witness how the interplay between these two forces has sculpted the contours of our world.

"The Power of Evidence: Decoding Facts and Authorities" seeks not only to inform but also to empower. In a time where the deluge of information can feel overwhelming, where truths can be obscured and falsehoods amplified, the need for a compass rooted in evidence is paramount. With each chapter, we will equip you with the tools to critically assess sources, distinguish between credible and dubious claims, and engage in meaningful discourse that bridges the gap between differing perspectives.

As we embark on this intellectual odyssey, let us embrace the uncertainty inherent in the pursuit of knowledge. Let us celebrate the capacity of evidence and authorities to illuminate our understanding, while remaining steadfast in our commitment to question, challenge, and refine our perceptions. "The Power of Evidence: Decoding Facts and Authorities" is an invitation to step beyond the surface of information, to engage with the intricate dance of truths and expertise that shapes our world. Together, we will unlock the transformative potential of evidence, affirming its role as a guiding force in our collective journey toward enlightenment.

TABLE OF CONTENTS

Topic 1: Cognitive Biases and the Interpretation of Facts

The human mind is a remarkable instrument of cognition, capable of intricate reasoning and profound insights. Yet, it is also susceptible to a range of cognitive biases – subtle, often unconscious mental shortcuts that can lead us astray in our interpretation of facts and authorities. In this exploration, we venture into the captivating realm of cognitive biases and their profound influence on how we perceive, process, and interpret information. Our journey takes us through the intricate web of biases, revealing their impact on decision-making, understanding, and the pursuit of truth.

The Nature of Cognitive Biases:

Diving into the foundation of cognitive biases, we uncover their evolutionary origins. These biases were once adaptive mechanisms that helped our ancestors make rapid decisions in life-threatening situations. However, in today's complex world, they can lead us to misjudge facts and authorities.

Cognitive biases, intricate patterns of thinking that influence how we process information and make decisions, offer a fascinating lens through which to explore the intricate workings of the human mind. Deep within these biases lie evolutionary origins that shed light on their adaptive purposes, while also revealing the potential pitfalls they present in our modern, complex world. By delving into the roots of cognitive biases, we uncover a rich tapestry of human psychology that informs our understanding of facts and authorities.

Evolutionary Foundations:

Cognitive biases, though often associated with errors in thinking, have their roots in the evolutionary history of our species. These biases evolved as efficient mental shortcuts that enabled our ancestors to make quick decisions in environments fraught with immediate dangers. For instance, the "fight or flight" response, triggered by the amygdala, is a primaeval survival mechanism that helped early humans react swiftly to potential threats. In this context, biases such as the confirmation bias and availability heuristic, which prioritise familiar and easily accessible information, were adaptive, allowing for rapid decision-making when milliseconds could mean the difference between life and death.

The Biases in Action:

In the modern world, where our environment has evolved significantly, these once-adaptive biases can lead to a disconnect between our intuitions and reality. The confirmation bias, which encourages us to seek out information that confirms our existing beliefs, can create echo chambers where alternative viewpoints are excluded. The availability heuristic, relying on readily available information, can distort our perception of the prevalence or importance of certain events. These biases shape how we interpret and remember facts, influencing our judgments of authorities and the information they present.

The Complexity of Modernity:

As our societies have grown more intricate and our challenges more multifaceted, cognitive biases that once offered efficiency now confront us with complexity. In the realm of facts and authorities, these biases can hinder objective evaluation and critical thinking. Our susceptibility to anchoring and adjustment bias, for example, might lead us to give undue weight to initial information when assessing an authority's credibility or a claim's validity. This can influence our perception of the evidence presented, altering our understanding of truth and expertise.

Navigating the Biases:

Understanding the evolutionary origins of cognitive biases provides a crucial foundation for addressing their influence in our lives. While these biases might have served us well in the past, a conscious awareness of their potential impact empowers us to navigate the complexities of the modern world with greater discernment. By cultivating critical thinking skills, practising mindfulness, and actively seeking out diverse perspectives, we can counteract the inherent tendencies of our cognitive biases. These strategies allow us to approach facts and authorities with a balanced perspective, engaging in a more meaningful and informed exploration of the truths that shape our understanding of the world.

In the intricate dance between our ancestral heritage and the challenges of the present, the nature of cognitive biases reveals both the strengths and vulnerabilities of human cognition. By acknowledging their historical significance and their implications for our interactions with facts and authorities, we embark on a journey of self-discovery and empowerment. As we unravel the layers of these biases, we equip ourselves to embrace a more nuanced, critical, and open-minded engagement with the power of evidence and the dynamics of expertise.

Confirmation Bias: The Reinforcement Trap:

One of the most pervasive biases, confirmation bias, shapes our tendency to seek out information that aligns with our preexisting beliefs. We explore its impact on our perception of facts and how it can create echo chambers, hindering our ability to consider alternative viewpoints.

Confirmation bias, a ubiquitous cognitive phenomenon deeply embedded in human psychology, exerts a profound influence on how we perceive, interpret, and interact with information. As a potent cognitive shortcut, confirmation bias leads us to selectively seek out, interpret, and remember information that supports our preexisting beliefs, while dismissing or downplaying information that contradicts them. This behavioural tendency has far-reaching implications for our understanding of facts, authorities, and the formation of beliefs, often leading to the creation of echo chambers – insular spaces where like-minded individuals reinforce each other's viewpoints and dissenting voices are marginalised.

The Mechanics of Confirmation Bias:

Confirmation bias operates beneath the surface of our conscious awareness, shaping our information-seeking behaviour and decision-making processes. When faced with new information, our brains naturally gravitate toward details that align with our existing beliefs. This bias subtly influences our perceptions, memory recall, and the conclusions we draw from evidence. Our brains prefer the comfort of affirmation over the discomfort of cognitive dissonance, leading us to prioritise information that confirms what we already know or believe.

The Reinforcement Trap:

At the heart of confirmation bias lies the reinforcement trap – a cycle where our initial beliefs are continually reinforced, often leading us further down the path of polarisation and cognitive rigidity. As we consistently expose ourselves to information that validates our existing perspectives, we inadvertently fortify our preconceived notions. This process can lead to a distorted sense of certainty, blinding us to alternative viewpoints and diminishing our ability to critically assess new evidence.

Echo Chambers and Polarisation:

Confirmation bias contributes to the formation of echo chambers, virtual spaces where individuals interact primarily with others who share similar beliefs. Within these chambers, confirmation bias collaborates with social media algorithms, news filters, and self-selection to create an environment that perpetuates homogeneity of thought. Instead of engaging in open dialogue and constructive debate, individuals in echo chambers reinforce each other's biases, resulting in a feedback loop of confirmation and a limited exposure to diverse perspectives.

Impact on Facts and Authorities:

Confirmation bias has a significant impact on our perception of facts and authorities. When we selectively seek information that supports our existing beliefs, we risk overlooking evidence that challenges or contradicts our assumptions. This bias can lead us to place undue trust in authorities that align with our views, potentially blinding us to the limitations or biases of those sources. As a consequence, we may unwittingly perpetuate misinformation and disinformation-related behaviours.

Mitigating Confirmation Bias: Strategies for Balanced Perception:

Recognizing and mitigating confirmation bias is crucial for maintaining a well-rounded, informed worldview.

Strategies such as seeking out diverse sources of information, deliberately engaging with dissenting viewpoints, and fostering a culture of open-mindedness can help counteract the reinforcement trap. Media literacy and critical thinking skills also play a vital role in empowering individuals to recognize and navigate the distortions caused by confirmation bias.

Availability Heuristic: The Power of Recent Information:

Delving into the availability heuristic, we uncover how the prominence of recent or easily accessible information can distort our assessment of facts. We examine how this bias can influence our perception of authorities and lead us to give more weight to information readily at hand.

The availability heuristic, a cognitive bias deeply ingrained in human thinking, offers a revealing glimpse into how our minds process information and make judgments.

This bias, driven by the accessibility and vividness of information, has a significant influence on our understanding of facts, authorities, and the world around us. By exploring the availability heuristic, we can unravel the complexities of its mechanisms, its impact on our perception of reality, and its role in shaping our interactions with authorities and information.

The Nature of the Availability Heuristic:

The availability heuristic operates on the principle that our minds tend to rely on information that is easily accessible or readily available when making decisions or forming opinions. When we can easily recall information from memory or when recent events are vivid in our minds, we tend to overestimate their significance and prevalence. This heuristic offers a mental shortcut, allowing us to make rapid judgments based on the information we can recall effortlessly.

Vividness and Accessibility: The Distortions of Perception

The availability heuristic hinges on the vividness of information – emotionally charged events or anecdotes tend to leave a more lasting impression, making them more accessible in our memory. This accessibility, however, does not always correlate with accuracy or representativeness. Our minds prioritise recent experiences or news stories, even if they are outliers, over more mundane or nuanced information.The availability heuristic, a cognitive bias, influences our decision-making by giving disproportionate weight to information that is vivid and easily accessible in our memory. This bias is rooted in the fact that emotionally charged events or anecdotes tend to leave a more lasting impression, making them more readily available when we need to make judgments or decisions. However, this accessibility doesn't always align with accuracy or representativeness, leading to distortions in our perception of reality.

The Role of Vividness in the Availability Heuristic:

Vividness refers to the quality of being clear, detailed, and emotionally impactful. Events or experiences that are vivid stand out in our minds due to their striking nature or emotional resonance. When making decisions, our minds tend to rely on these vivid memories as shortcuts to judge the likelihood or significance of events.

Impact on Accessibility and Decision-Making:

Vivid information is more accessible in our memory, making it easier to retrieve and use when making judgments. However, this accessibility doesn't necessarily correlate with the accuracy or representativeness of the information. Our minds prioritise vivid examples, anecdotes, or emotionally charged events, even if they are outliers or rare occurrences, over more mundane or nuanced information.

The Influence of Recentness:

The availability heuristic is also influenced by the recentness of an experience or the recency of exposure to information. Recent events are more accessible in our memory and thus have a stronger impact on our decision-making. This can lead to skewed judgments, as we tend to overestimate the prevalence or likelihood of events that have recently captured our attention, even if they are not representative of the broader context.

Bias in Perceptions and Decisions:

The availability heuristic can lead to biassed perceptions and decisions. For example, if we encounter a series of news stories about plane crashes, our perception of the safety of air travel might be disproportionately negative, even though statistically, flying is one of the safest modes of transportation. This bias can also affect how we assess risks, make financial decisions, or form opinions on various issues.

Mitigating the Impact:

To mitigate the distortions caused by the availability heuristic, individuals need to be aware of its influence and take deliberate steps to critically assess the information they encounter. This involves seeking out diverse sources, fact-checking emotionally charged anecdotes, and considering the broader context rather than relying solely on what is most vivid and accessible in memory.

The Power of Recent Information:

Recent information carries a weight of immediacy that can distort our assessment of facts and authorities. The news cycle inundated us with fresh information, and the human tendency to give prominence to the most recent data can lead us to form skewed perceptions. The availability of recent information can create a temporal bias, where events that happened more recently feel more significant than those in the past, regardless of their actual impact.

Influence on Perception of Authorities:

The availability heuristic also extends to our perception of authorities. We may unconsciously assign greater credibility to individuals or sources that are more prominently featured in recent discussions or media coverage. The visibility of an authority figure in current discourse can lead us to attribute greater expertise to them, potentially overshadowing other voices that might hold equally or more valid perspectives.

Navigating the Bias: Strategies for Balanced Perception:

Recognizing the power of the availability heuristic is the first step in mitigating its impact. Engaging in critical thinking and media literacy allows us to question the biases that this heuristic introduces. Deliberate efforts to seek out diverse sources of information, historical context, and statistical data can counteract the distortions caused by the heuristic's focus on recent or vivid examples.

Anchoring and Adjustment: The Influence of Initial Reference Points:

Anchoring bias, a cognitive bias that anchors our decisions to initial pieces of information, affects our interpretation of

facts and authorities. We analyse how this bias can lead to inaccurate judgments and explore strategies to mitigate its effects.
The Illusion of Control and Overconfidence:

Unpacking the illusion of control and overconfidence biases, we discuss their impact on our assessment of facts and authorities. We delve into how these biases can lead to unwarranted certainty and examine the implications for decision-making.
Strategies for Mitigating Cognitive Biases:

We provide practical strategies for recognizing and counteracting cognitive biases. From cultivating mindfulness and critical thinking skills to seeking diverse perspectives, we empower readers to navigate the intricate landscape of biases and enhance their interpretation of facts.
Technology and Cognitive Biases:

In the digital age, technology both amplifies and interacts with cognitive biases. We explore how algorithms and personalised content feeds can exacerbate biases, contributing to the spread of misinformation. Additionally, we discuss the potential of technology to mitigate biases through innovative tools and platforms.

Topic 2: Authority in a Post-Truth Era

In an era characterised by the rapid dissemination of information and the democratisation of knowledge, the concept of authority has undergone a profound transformation. The traditional gatekeepers of information, such as established institutions and experts, now contend with a cacophony of voices vying for attention in an ever-expanding digital landscape. As we navigate this dynamic terrain, we delve into the multifaceted dimensions of authority in a post-truth era. Our exploration uncovers the challenges posed by misinformation, the erosion of trust, and the critical role that media literacy and critical thinking play in discerning credible sources of information.

The Shifting Landscape of Authority:

We begin by examining the historical role of traditional authorities – institutions, experts, and renowned figures – as custodians of knowledge and arbiters of truth. We then delve into the seismic shifts caused by the digital age, where anyone with an internet connection can broadcast their views, blurring the lines between expertise and opinion.

The availability heuristic, a cognitive bias deeply ingrained in human thinking, offers a revealing glimpse into how our minds process information and make judgments. This bias, driven by the accessibility and vividness of information, has a significant influence on our understanding of facts, authorities, and the world around us. By exploring the availability heuristic, we can unravel the complexities of its mechanisms, its impact on our perception of reality, and its role in shaping our interactions with authorities and information.

The Nature of the Availability Heuristic:

The availability heuristic operates on the principle that our minds tend to rely on information that is easily accessible or readily available when making decisions or forming opinions. When we can easily recall information from memory or when recent events are vivid in our minds, we tend to overestimate their significance and prevalence. This heuristic offers a mental shortcut, allowing us to make rapid judgments based on the information we can recall effortlessly.

Vividness and Accessibility: The Distortions of Perception:

The availability heuristic hinges on the vividness of information – emotionally charged events or anecdotes tend to leave a more lasting impression, making them more accessible in our memory. This accessibility, however, does not always correlate with accuracy or representativeness. Our minds prioritise recent experiences or news stories, even if they are outliers, over more mundane or nuanced information.

The Power of Recent Information:

Recent information carries a weight of immediacy that can distort our assessment of facts and authorities. The news cycle inundated us with fresh information, and the human tendency to give prominence to the most recent data can lead us to form skewed perceptions. The availability of recent information can create a temporal bias, where events that happened more recently feel more significant than those in the past, regardless of their actual impact.

Influence on Perception of Authorities:

The availability heuristic also extends to our perception of authorities. We may unconsciously assign greater credibility to individuals or sources that are more prominently featured in recent discussions or media coverage. The visibility of an authority figure in current discourse can lead us to attribute greater expertise to them, potentially overshadowing other voices that might hold equally or more valid perspectives.

Navigating the Bias: Strategies for Balanced Perception:

Recognizing the power of the availability heuristic is the first step in mitigating its impact. Engaging in critical thinking and media literacy allows us to question the biases that this heuristic introduces. Deliberate efforts to seek out diverse sources of information, historical context, and statistical data can counteract the distortions caused by the heuristic's focus on recent or vivid examples.

The Rise of Misinformation:

Investigating the proliferation of misinformation, we dissect how false or misleading information spreads through social media, echo chambers, and viral content. We delve into case studies that highlight the social, political, and economic ramifications of misinformation, emphasising the need for vigilance.
The rise of misinformation stands as a formidable challenge in the digital age, reshaping the way we perceive facts, authorities, and the truth itself. Investigating the proliferation of misinformation reveals a complex landscape of false or misleading information that spreads like wildfire through the interconnected realms of social media, echo chambers, and viral content. Delving into this phenomenon, we unravel the mechanisms behind its propagation, its profound social, political, and economic ramifications, and the urgent need for

vigilant discernment in an era of unprecedented information access.

The Mechanisms of Misinformation Spread:

Misinformation thrives in the digital age due to its swift dissemination through various channels. Social media platforms, designed to connect individuals, inadvertently amplify the reach of false information. Algorithms often prioritise sensational and polarising content, leading to the rapid spread of clickbait headlines and dubious claims. Echo chambers, fueled by confirmation bias, reinforce preexisting beliefs, further amplifying the misinformation within these insular communities. Viral content, often designed for emotional impact, spreads rapidly as users share sensational stories without fact-checking.

Case Studies: Unmasking the Impact:

Real-world case studies vividly illustrate the consequences of misinformation. From health-related hoaxes that fuel scepticism about vaccines to politically motivated falsehoods that manipulate public opinion, misinformation disrupts public discourse, undermines trust in institutions, and fuels societal divisions. The "Pizzagate" conspiracy theory and the spread of false information during natural disasters demonstrate how misinformation can have severe consequences, from threats to individuals' safety to the erosion of societal cohesion.

The Social, Political, and Economic Ramifications:

The ramifications of misinformation extend beyond the realm of information itself. Misinformation can influence elections, polarise communities, and even lead to violence. The proliferation of false information can erode trust in traditional authorities and media sources, contributing to the fragmentation of shared reality. Economically, misinformation can damage the reputations of businesses, cause stock market fluctuations, and impact consumer behaviours. The costs of misinformation are felt across the spectrum of society, from individuals to governments to global institutions.

The Need for Vigilance and Media Literacy:

In the face of the misinformation epidemic, cultivating media literacy and critical thinking becomes paramount. Navigating the digital landscape demands an informed approach, where individuals assess information for credibility, verify claims through trusted sources, and discern fact from fiction. Engaging with diverse viewpoints, questioning sources, and sharing information responsibly are essential steps to curbing the spread of misinformation.

Erosion of Trust and Distrust of Authorities:

We analyse the factors contributing to the erosion of trust in traditional authorities, from instances of institutional failure to allegations of bias and corruption. Exploring the psychology of trust, we illuminate the complex relationship between scepticism, cynicism, and the quest for credible sources. The erosion of trust in traditional authorities stands as a defining feature of our contemporary society, fundamentally reshaping the way we engage with information, experts, and institutions. Analysing the multifaceted factors contributing to this erosion reveals a landscape marked by instances of institutional failure, allegations of bias and corruption, and a growing disconnection between authority figures and the public they serve. Exploring the psychology of trust illuminates the intricate dance between scepticism, cynicism, and the pursuit of credible sources in an age where trust is both essential and elusive.

Institutional Failures and Credibility Deficits:

The erosion of trust is often fueled by high-profile instances of institutional failure. Scandals, cover-ups, and mishandling of crises have led the public to question the motives and competence of once-revered authorities. Whether in politics, healthcare, or finance, these failures have far-reaching implications, eroding the foundation upon which trust in authorities is built.

Allegations of Bias and Corruption

Distrust of authorities is compounded by allegations of bias and corruption. Media outlets, once seen as unbiased purveyors of information, now face scrutiny for potential political leanings or sensationalism. Accusations of corporate influence on scientific research or government officials' manipulation of information can lead to perceptions of authorities as unreliable sources, driving individuals to seek alternative perspectives.Allegations of bias and corruption play a significant role in eroding trust in traditional authorities, whether they be media outlets, institutions, or government bodies. These allegations stem from concerns about the objectivity, integrity, and transparency of the information provided by these authorities. As public discourse and information dissemination become increasingly complex, the scrutiny of potential bias and corruption amplifies, leading to a widespread scepticism that can have far-reaching consequences.

Media Outlets Under the Lens:

Media outlets, once regarded as objective and neutral sources of information, are now subject to intense scrutiny due to allegations of bias. These allegations arise from perceptions that media organisations are influenced by political agendas, commercial interests, or sensationalism. In an era of highly polarised political landscapes, media outlets are often accused of catering to specific audiences, leading to concerns about their impartiality and credibility.

Corporate Influence and Scientific Research:

Accusations of corporate influence on scientific research raise questions about the objectivity of information presented to the public. When research studies are funded by corporations with vested interests, there's potential for bias in study design, data interpretation, and reporting. This can undermine the credibility of scientific findings, especially when financial motivations are perceived to overshadow the pursuit of unbiased knowledge.

Government Manipulation of Information

Government authorities are not immune to allegations of bias and manipulation. When officials selectively present information to further political agendas or downplay certain aspects of an issue, the credibility of the information is compromised. This manipulation of information can foster a climate of distrust, making it difficult for the public to discern objective truth from political spin.In the realm of information and authority, even government institutions are susceptible to allegations of bias and manipulation. When officials selectively present information to advance political agendas or deliberately downplay certain facets of an issue, the integrity and credibility of the information itself come under scrutiny. This manipulation of information not only distorts public perception but also undermines trust in institutions, creating an environment where discerning objective truth from political spin becomes increasingly challenging.

Selective Presentation for Political Agenda:

Government manipulation of information can take the form of selectively highlighting certain aspects of a story while suppressing or omitting others. This strategic presentation aims to influence public opinion in favour of a particular political narrative. By focusing on specific data points or framing issues in a particular way, authorities can shape how the public perceives events or policies.

Downplaying Contradictory Information:

Another tactic involves downplaying or dismissing information that contradicts the desired narrative. Officials may choose to ignore data or expert opinions that challenge their position, creating an environment where dissenting viewpoints are marginalised. This not only distorts the information landscape but also prevents the public from receiving a complete and balanced understanding of complex issues.

Impact on Credibility and Trust:

When government authorities manipulate information, the credibility of the information itself is compromised. The public expects accurate, unbiased, and transparent communication from government sources. When this expectation is not met, trust in institutions erodes, leading to scepticism about the veracity of the information presented. This erosion of trust has far-reaching implications, affecting public discourse, decision-making, and overall governance.

Climate of Distrust:

Manipulation of information fosters a climate of distrust, where citizens become increasingly sceptical of official pronouncements. As allegations of bias and manipulation persist, individuals may begin to question the motives behind government communication. This climate of distrust hampers the ability of authorities to effectively communicate with the public and gain support for policies or initiatives.

Challenges in Discerning Truth:

The manipulation of information by government authorities poses challenges for the public in discerning objective truth. With information presented through a political lens, citizens must navigate a landscape where facts are intertwined with strategic messaging. This complexity can lead to confusion, apathy, and a sense of disillusionment, making it difficult to make informed decisions based on reliable information.

Impact on Trust and Perception:

Allegations of bias and corruption erode trust in authorities by casting doubt on their intentions and motivations. When individuals perceive that information is being manipulated to serve ulterior motives, they become sceptical of the authenticity and reliability of the information presented. This scepticism extends beyond the specific instances of bias and corruption, influencing how individuals approach information from other sources as well.

Seeking Alternative Perspectives:

As a consequence of allegations of bias and corruption, individuals may actively seek alternative perspectives to verify information. This search for independent validation can lead to a fragmentation of information sources, as individuals turn to sources that align with their existing beliefs or that present counter arguments. While seeking diverse perspectives can be healthy, an overemphasis on alternative sources can contribute to echo chambers and further polarise public discourse.

In response to allegations of bias and corruption within traditional sources of information, individuals often adopt a proactive approach by seeking alternative perspectives to validate the information they receive. This pursuit of independent validation is driven by a desire for a more well-rounded understanding and a safeguard against misinformation. However, this practice can lead to unintended consequences, including a fragmentation of information sources, the reinforcement of existing beliefs, and the potential for echo chambers that polarise public discourse.

The Search for Independent Validation:

When faced with allegations of bias or corruption within traditional authorities, individuals may feel compelled to seek out corroborating information from alternative sources. This practice is rooted in a healthy scepticism that encourages individuals to critically evaluate information rather than accepting it at face value. Seeking diverse viewpoints can serve as a safeguard against misinformation and manipulation.

Fragmentation of Information Sources:

While seeking alternative perspectives can be constructive, an overemphasis on diversification can lead to a fragmentation of information sources. Individuals may gravitate towards sources that confirm their existing beliefs or support counterarguments, unintentionally isolating themselves within specific ideological bubbles. This fragmentation can hinder a comprehensive understanding of complex issues by limiting exposure to a narrow range of viewpoints.

Reinforcement of Existing Beliefs:

The pursuit of alternative perspectives can paradoxically reinforce existing beliefs. Individuals are more likely to seek out sources that align with their preexisting opinions, which can reinforce confirmation bias – the tendency to favour information that confirms what one already believes. This selective exposure can hinder intellectual growth and impede the ability to engage with viewpoints that challenge one's own.

Echo Chambers and Polarisation:

The aggregation of individuals who share similar viewpoints within specific information bubbles creates echo chambers. In these insulated environments, confirmation bias is magnified, leading to the entrenchment of polarised opinions. Echo chambers hinder meaningful dialogue, as individuals are shielded from diverse perspectives that could broaden their understanding and encourage a more nuanced discourse.

Balancing Diversity with Critical Engagement:

While seeking alternative perspectives is crucial for a well-informed citizenry, it is equally important to approach this practice with discernment and critical thinking. Rather than solely relying on sources that confirm existing beliefs, individuals should actively engage with viewpoints that challenge their assumptions. Engaging in thoughtful analysis of differing perspectives can prevent the reinforcement of biases and encourage a more open-minded and inclusive discourse.

Restoring Trust and Transparency:

Addressing allegations of bias and corruption requires authorities to demonstrate transparency, ethical conduct, and a commitment to serving the public interest. Media outlets must uphold journalistic integrity and provide balanced coverage. Institutions must implement measures to prevent conflicts of interest in research and decision-making. Governments should prioritise open communication and accurate information dissemination to rebuild trust.

Addressing allegations of bias and corruption is essential for restoring trust in authorities, whether they are media outlets, institutions, or governments. To regain credibility and foster public confidence, these entities must demonstrate transparency, ethical conduct, and a genuine commitment to serving the public interest. By upholding journalistic integrity, implementing measures to prevent conflicts of interest, and prioritising open communication, trust can be rebuilt, and transparency can become a cornerstone of their operations.

Media Outlets: Upholding Journalistic Integrity

Media outlets play a pivotal role in restoring trust by upholding journalistic principles. This involves reporting news accurately, objectively, and without sensationalism. Fact-checking, verification of sources, and providing comprehensive context are essential to prevent the spread of misinformation. Clear delineation between news and opinion content is crucial to maintaining credibility and ensuring that personal biases do not seep into reporting.

Institutions: Preventing Conflicts of Interest

Institutions, whether in academia or other sectors, must take measures to prevent conflicts of interest that could compromise their objectivity. Transparent disclosure of funding sources, affiliations, and potential biases is vital. Implementing rigorous peer review processes and adhering to ethical guidelines help ensure that research and decision-making remain untainted by external pressures.

Governments: Prioritising Open Communication

Governments play a central role in restoring trust by prioritising open communication and accurate information dissemination. Transparency in policy-making, sharing data and evidence, and addressing concerns openly contribute to a sense of accountability. Avoiding manipulation of information for political gain and being responsive to citizen inquiries help rebuild trust in the government's commitment to serving the public.

The Role of Technology: Leveraging Digital Tools

In the digital age, technology can play a crucial role in enhancing transparency. Governments and institutions can leverage digital platforms to provide real-time updates, share data, and engage with the public. Media outlets can utilise interactive features to provide additional context and sources for their stories, fostering a deeper understanding among their audience.

Rebuilding Credibility: A Collaborative Effort

Restoring trust and transparency requires a collaborative effort among media outlets, institutions, governments, and the public. Authorities need to take proactive steps to address allegations of bias and corruption, demonstrate accountability, and actively engage with feedback from the public. In turn, the public's critical engagement and demand for transparent information drive these entities to maintain high standards of credibility and integrity.

The Complex Psychology of Trust

The psychology of trust is a complex interplay of cognitive processes, emotions, and social dynamics. Trust is built on a delicate balance of competence, integrity, and benevolence. When any of these components are compromised, scepticism arises. However, a healthy dose of scepticism can evolve into cynicism when individuals consistently perceive authorities as untrustworthy or self-serving.Trust, a fundamental aspect of human interactions, is a complex psychological construct that involves a delicate interplay of cognitive processes, emotions, and social dynamics. It forms the foundation of relationships, institutions, and societal cohesion. Yet, the psychology of trust is multifaceted, shaped by factors ranging from competence and integrity to emotional responses and past experiences. Understanding the intricate mechanisms behind trust is essential for comprehending its formation, maintenance, and potential erosion.

Components of Trust: Competence, Integrity, and Benevolence

Trust is built upon a tripod of essential components – competence, integrity, and benevolence. Individuals place trust in authorities when they perceive them as competent, possessing the expertise and capability to fulfil their roles effectively. Integrity, the alignment of actions with values and principles, is another crucial aspect; when authorities act consistently with their stated intentions, trust flourishes. Benevolence, or the belief that authorities have the best interests of individuals at heart, further solidifies the foundation of trust.

The Erosion of Trust: Compromised Components

When any of the components of trust are compromised, scepticism emerges. Instances of incompetence, dishonesty, or self-interest can trigger doubt in the authenticity of authorities. The erosion of trust often occurs incrementally, stemming from repeated experiences of unmet expectations or perceived breaches of trust. A single event might not be enough to shatter trust, but a pattern of behaviour can significantly undermine it.

Scepticism vs. Cynicism: A Fine Line

A healthy dose of scepticism is a rational response to potential threats to trust. It encourages critical evaluation, fact-checking, and cautious decision-making. However, when individuals consistently perceive authorities as untrustworthy or self-serving, scepticism can evolve into cynicism. Cynicism reflects a deep-seated belief that authorities are inherently untrustworthy and motivations are driven solely by self-interest. Cynicism often leads to a loss of faith in institutions, creating a barrier to constructive engagement.

Emotional Dimensions: Fear, Hope, and Betrayal

The psychology of trust is intertwined with emotions. Fear of betrayal can lead individuals to become cautious, reluctant to place trust in authorities out of a fear of disappointment. Hope, on the other hand, motivates individuals to give authorities the benefit of the doubt and maintain a positive outlook. A breach of trust can evoke feelings of betrayal and anger, leading to a profound erosion of trust that may take time to heal.

Rebuilding Trust: Transparency and Consistency

Restoring trust requires a combination of transparency and consistency. Transparent communication helps bridge the gap between perceived intentions and actual actions, demonstrating that authorities are forthright in their motives. Consistency in behaviour and decision-making reaffirms the trustworthiness of authorities. However, rebuilding trust is a gradual process that demands sustained effort to address the root causes of scepticism or cynicism.Trust, a fundamental aspect of human interactions, is a complex psychological construct that involves a delicate interplay of cognitive processes, emotions, and social dynamics. It forms the foundation of relationships, institutions, and societal cohesion. Yet, the psychology of trust is multifaceted, shaped by factors ranging from competence and integrity to emotional responses and past experiences. Understanding the intricate mechanisms behind trust is essential for comprehending its formation, maintenance, and potential erosion.

Components of Trust: Competence, Integrity, and Benevolence

Trust is built upon a tripod of essential components – competence, integrity, and benevolence. Individuals place trust in authorities when they perceive them as competent, possessing the expertise and capability to fulfil their roles effectively. Integrity, the alignment of actions with values and principles, is another crucial aspect; when authorities act consistently with their stated intentions, trust flourishes. Benevolence, or the belief that authorities have the best interests of individuals at heart, further solidifies the foundation of trust.

The Erosion of Trust: Compromised Components

When any of the components of trust are compromised, scepticism emerges. Instances of incompetence, dishonesty, or self-interest can trigger doubt in the authenticity of authorities. The erosion of trust often occurs incrementally, stemming from repeated experiences of unmet expectations or perceived breaches of trust. A single event might not be enough to shatter trust, but a pattern of behaviour can significantly undermine it.

Scepticism vs. Cynicism: A Fine Line

A healthy dose of scepticism is a rational response to potential threats to trust. It encourages critical evaluation, fact-checking, and cautious decision-making. However, when individuals consistently perceive authorities as untrustworthy or self-serving, scepticism can evolve into cynicism. Cynicism reflects a deep-seated belief that authorities are inherently untrustworthy and motivations are driven solely by self-interest. Cynicism often leads to a loss of faith in institutions, creating a barrier to constructive engagement.

Emotional Dimensions: Fear, Hope, and Betrayal

The psychology of trust is intertwined with emotions. Fear of betrayal can lead individuals to become cautious, reluctant to place trust in authorities out of a fear of disappointment. Hope, on the other hand, motivates individuals to give authorities the benefit of the doubt and maintain a positive outlook. A breach of trust can evoke feelings of betrayal and anger, leading to a profound erosion of trust that may take time to heal.

Rebuilding Trust: Transparency and Consistency

Restoring trust requires a combination of transparency and consistency. Transparent communication helps bridge the gap between perceived intentions and actual actions, demonstrating that authorities are forthright in their motives. Consistency in behaviour and decision-making reaffirms the trustworthiness of authorities. However, rebuilding trust is a gradual process that demands sustained effort to address the root causes of scepticism or cynicism.

Scepticism, Cynicism, and the Quest for Credible Sources

Scepticism, born out of critical thinking and vigilance, serves as a protective mechanism against misinformation and manipulation. However, an overabundance of scepticism can breed cynicism, leading individuals to reject all sources of information as biassed or untrustworthy. The challenge lies in finding a middle ground – a space where scepticism coexists with openness to credible information from reliable sources.

In the quest for accurate information and a trustworthy understanding of the world, individuals often navigate a spectrum that ranges from scepticism to cynicism. These psychological attitudes reflect how we engage with the information presented to us and the authorities that disseminate it. Striking the right balance between scepticism, cynicism, and the pursuit of credible sources is pivotal for informed decision-making, responsible engagement, and maintaining a healthy information landscape.

Scepticism: A Guardian of Critical Thinking

Scepticism is rooted in the principles of critical thinking and vigilance. It encourages individuals to question claims, evaluate evidence, and seek reliable sources before accepting information as true. Scepticism acts as a protective mechanism against misinformation, manipulation, and unwarranted assumptions. By applying a critical lens to information, individuals are empowered to make well-informed decisions and avoid falling victim to deceptive narratives.

Cynicism: The Pitfall of Excessive Scepticism

While scepticism is a valuable tool, an overabundance of it can evolve into cynicism. Cynicism reflects a deep-seated distrust of information sources, institutions, and authorities. It arises when individuals consistently view information through a lens of suspicion, assuming that all sources are inherently biassed or untrustworthy. Cynicism can lead to disengagement, apathy, and a refusal to engage with information altogether, creating an environment where constructive dialogue becomes challenging.

The Middle Ground: Navigating Scepticism and Openness

The challenge lies in finding a middle ground where scepticism coexists with openness to credible sources. This balance allows individuals to critically evaluate information while remaining receptive to evidence-based viewpoints. Recognizing that no source is entirely free from bias, individuals can apply scepticism selectively, focusing on evaluating the credibility of sources based on their track record, transparency, and adherence to journalistic or academic standards.

The Importance of Discernment:

Navigating scepticism and openness requires discernment – the ability to judge the reliability and credibility of sources. Discernment involves evaluating the expertise of authors, cross-referencing information, and considering the context in which information is presented. Developing discernment skills enables individuals to differentiate between well-researched, evidence-based content and sensationalist or misleading narratives.

Building a Foundation of Trust:

Ultimately, the goal is to build a foundation of trust in credible sources while maintaining a healthy dose of scepticism. Engaging with information sources that prioritise accuracy, transparency, and ethical reporting fosters a sense of trust. At the same time, practising scepticism by questioning claims, seeking diverse viewpoints, and fact-checking contributes to a more responsible, well-rounded approach to information consumption.

Rebuilding Trust: Strategies and Challenges:

Rebuilding trust requires a multifaceted approach. Authorities must engage in transparent communication, acknowledge mistakes, and demonstrate a commitment to ethical conduct. Media outlets must uphold journalistic integrity and navigate the complexities of unbiased reporting. Individuals play a vital role by seeking out credible sources, questioning assumptions, and fostering a culture of critical thinking.

Media Literacy and Critical Thinking:

Addressing the urgency of media literacy, we equip readers with strategies to navigate the digital landscape. We explore the art of discerning credible sources, evaluating information for bias, and fostering critical thinking skills that empower individuals to distinguish fact from fiction.

In an era characterised by the constant flow of information from diverse sources, the skills of media literacy and critical thinking have risen to paramount importance. The digital landscape, with its flood of news, opinions, and claims, demands that individuals become savvy navigators –

equipped to discern credible sources from misinformation, evaluate information for bias, and cultivate the ability to think critically about the world around them. Addressing the urgency of media literacy, we delve into the strategies that empower individuals to navigate the vast digital seas of information with wisdom, discernment, and intellectual integrity.

The Digital Information Ecosystem:

The digital age has transformed the way we consume and disseminate information. With a plethora of platforms, voices, and perspectives available at our fingertips, the challenge lies in distinguishing between reliable information and biassed or false claims. Media literacy acts as a compass, guiding us through this intricate ecosystem.

The Art of Discerning Credible Sources:

One of the foundational pillars of media literacy is the ability to discern credible sources. Individuals must be equipped with the skills to evaluate the reputation of publishers, authors, and organisations. Scrutinising the author's credentials, assessing the credibility of the platform, and considering potential conflicts of interest are all essential steps in determining the reliability of a source.

Evaluating Information for Bias and Objectivity

Media literacy extends beyond identifying credible sources; it also involves evaluating information for bias and objectivity. The ability to recognize the subtle ways in which bias can infiltrate news coverage or persuasive arguments is a critical skill. Engaging with content that presents multiple viewpoints and seeking out diverse perspectives can help individuals develop a more comprehensive understanding of complex issues.

In the digital age, media literacy encompasses more than simply discerning credible sources; it entails the crucial skill of evaluating information for bias and objectivity. This skill is paramount in a world inundated with information, where individuals must navigate a complex web of narratives, opinions, and perspectives. The ability to recognize and dissect the subtle ways in which bias can seep into news coverage, persuasive arguments, and even seemingly objective content is a foundational component of informed citizenship and critical thinking.

The Nature of Bias:

Bias, inherent in human perception, is an inclination towards particular perspectives or interpretations that stem from personal beliefs, cultural influences, or ideological leanings. In media and information dissemination, bias can manifest in various forms, such as framing, selection of sources, and word choice. Understanding that no piece of information is entirely neutral empowers individuals to approach content with a discerning eye.

Recognizing Bias in News Coverage:

Evaluating news coverage for bias involves examining how stories are framed, the language used, and the sources cited. Bias can be implicit, stemming from journalists' perspectives or systemic editorial decisions. By comparing multiple news sources on the same topic, individuals can gain insight into how different outlets present information, allowing them to identify patterns and potential biases.

Unmasking Bias in Persuasive Content:

Persuasive content, including opinion pieces, advertisements, and advocacy materials, often carries inherent bias. Recognizing persuasive intent requires dissecting the rhetorical strategies employed, assessing the evidence presented, and understanding the underlying motivations. Individuals can critically evaluate whether the content is based on sound reasoning and evidence or if it manipulates emotions to influence opinions.

Cultivating Objectivity through Diverse Perspectives:

While complete objectivity might be unattainable, a commitment to balance and diversity of perspectives contributes to a more comprehensive understanding of complex issues. Engaging with content that presents various viewpoints, even those that challenge one's own beliefs, fosters critical thinking. This approach enables individuals to weigh different arguments, assess evidence, and draw informed conclusions.

Seeking Diverse Voices:

Media literacy involves actively seeking out diverse voices and perspectives to counteract the echo chamber effect – the tendency to consume information that reaffirms preexisting beliefs. Exploring content from different ideological backgrounds, cultural perspectives, and demographic representations expands one's understanding and nurtures empathy and open-mindedness.

Empowerment through Critical Engagement:

Evaluating information for bias and objectivity empowers individuals to engage critically with the information they encounter. This skill is a vital safeguard against manipulation, misinformation, and the reinforcement of one's own biases. By honing the ability to distinguish between factual reporting and opinion, individuals can make well-informed decisions and contribute to a more informed, engaged, and pluralistic society.

The Role of Critical Thinking

Critical thinking serves as the foundation upon which media literacy is built. It empowers individuals to question assumptions, analyse evidence, and consider alternative explanations. Encouraging critical thinking involves fostering curiosity, encouraging scepticism, and teaching individuals to approach information with an open yet discerning mind.Critical thinking stands as the cornerstone of media literacy, forming the bedrock upon which informed decision-making, responsible engagement, and a discerning understanding of information rest. In an era where information flows ceaselessly and the boundaries between fact and fiction blur, the ability to critically assess, analyse, and interpret information is an indispensable skill that equips individuals to navigate the complexities of the digital age.

The Essence of Critical Thinking:

Critical thinking involves a deliberate, reflective approach to information. It empowers individuals to move beyond passive consumption and toward active engagement. It entails questioning assumptions, challenging narratives, and rigorously evaluating the evidence presented. In essence, critical thinking encourages a journey from merely accepting information to examining it with a discerning and analytical eye.

Questioning Assumptions:

At its core, critical thinking compels individuals to question assumptions – those underlying beliefs or biases that shape how information is interpreted. By recognizing the influence of assumptions, individuals can avoid falling into the trap of accepting information uncritically. This practice not only allows for more accurate assessments but also opens the door to considering alternative viewpoints.

Analysing Evidence:

Central to critical thinking is the ability to analyse evidence. Individuals learn to assess the quality, credibility, and relevance of the sources supporting a claim. This process involves evaluating the methodology, objectivity, and expertise behind the evidence presented. By scrutinising evidence, critical thinkers can distinguish between well-substantiated claims and those lacking substantial support.

Embracing Curiosity and Scepticism:

Critical thinking thrives on curiosity and scepticism. Curiosity compels individuals to explore beyond the surface, delve deeper into topics, and seek out diverse perspectives. Scepticism, when applied judiciously, encourages individuals to question the veracity of claims, probe for hidden motivations, and demand transparent and robust evidence.

Balancing Open-Mindedness with Discernment:

Critical thinking strikes a balance between open-mindedness and discernment. It encourages individuals to approach information with an open mind, willing to consider new ideas and viewpoints. However, this openness is tempered by the need for discernment – the ability to evaluate information rigorously and differentiate between well-supported arguments and unsubstantiated claims.

Teaching Critical Thinking: Nurturing Informed Citizens

Promoting critical thinking involves fostering its principles from an early age. Education systems and curricula play a pivotal role in nurturing this skill. Encouraging students to engage in discussions, analyse diverse sources, and question assumptions instils a habit of mind that lasts a lifetime. Encouraging media literacy education equips individuals with tools to navigate the complex information landscape responsibly.

Strategies for Nurturing Critical Thinking

Nurturing critical thinking requires intentional efforts. Encouraging individuals to ask probing questions, examine the reliability of sources, fact-check claims, and assess the logical coherence of arguments are all strategies that can help cultivate a habit of thoughtful analysis.Nurturing critical thinking is a deliberate endeavour that empowers individuals to navigate the complexities of the modern information landscape with discernment and wisdom. By incorporating intentional strategies into education, media consumption, and everyday interactions, we can foster a culture of thoughtful analysis that equips individuals to question assumptions, evaluate evidence, and engage with information responsibly.

1. Encourage Questioning:

The foundation of critical thinking lies in the art of asking probing questions. Encourage individuals to question assumptions, challenge claims, and explore the underlying motivations behind the information presented. By nurturing a curious and inquisitive mindset, individuals become more adept at uncovering hidden biases, inconsistencies, and potential gaps in reasoning.

2. Evaluate Source Reliability:

Teach individuals to assess the reliability of sources. Encourage them to consider the expertise, reputation, and objectivity of the authors or organisations providing the information. Discuss the importance of peer review, reputable publications, and recognized experts in various fields as markers of reliable sources.

3. Fact-Check Claims:

Empower individuals to fact-check claims before accepting them as true. Highlight the significance of cross-referencing information from multiple credible sources and consulting fact-checking organisations. Showcasing examples of how misinformation spreads and the consequences of believing false claims can underscore the importance of rigorous fact-checking.

4. Analyse Logical Coherence:

Help individuals develop the skill of assessing the logical coherence of arguments. Teach them to identify logical fallacies, faulty reasoning, and weak evidence that undermine the credibility of claims. Equipping individuals with the ability to identify flawed arguments enhances their capacity to engage with information critically.

5. Practise Socratic Dialogue:

Engage in Socratic dialogue – a method of questioning that stimulates critical thinking through thoughtful conversations. Encourage individuals to engage in discussions where they must articulate their viewpoints, defend their positions, and respond to counter arguments. This process encourages them to think deeply about their beliefs, consider alternative viewpoints, and refine their understanding.

6. Embrace Multidisciplinary Learning:

Expose individuals to a variety of disciplines and perspectives. Encouraging multidisciplinary learning broadens their horizons and helps them appreciate how different fields approach problems, analyse evidence, and construct arguments. Exposure to diverse perspectives nurtures a well-rounded critical thinker capable of synthesising information from various sources.

7. Provide Real-Life Examples:

Offer real-life examples that illustrate the consequences of uncritical thinking. Showcase instances where misinformation led to detrimental outcomes and instances where critical thinking helped individuals make informed decisions. By connecting theory with practical implications, individuals can understand the tangible impact of their critical thinking skills.

8. Foster Media Literacy:

Media literacy education is instrumental in nurturing critical thinking. Teach individuals to navigate media landscapes, identify bias, assess credibility, and differentiate between factual reporting and opinion pieces. Equip them with tools to engage with digital media responsibly, distinguishing reliable sources from sensationalism and misinformation.

9. Create a Safe Environment:

Foster an environment where individuals feel safe to question, express doubt, and engage in respectful discussions. Encouraging a culture that values thoughtful analysis rather than blind conformity empowers individuals to exercise their critical thinking skills without fear of judgement.

Educational Imperative and Lifelong Learning

Media literacy and critical thinking are not skills confined to a single educational stage; they are lifelong tools for informed engagement. Educational institutions, families, and communities all play a role in instilling these skills. Additionally, the digital landscape evolves rapidly, necessitating ongoing learning and adaptation to new platforms and information-sharing mechanisms.Media literacy and critical thinking are not just skills limited to a specific educational stage; they are essential tools that extend throughout an individual's lifetime. In an era characterised by an overwhelming influx of information and rapidly changing technological landscapes, cultivating these skills becomes an educational imperative that spans across educational institutions, families, communities, and personal pursuits.

The Lifelong Nature of Media Literacy:

Media literacy and critical thinking are not learned once and forgotten. Instead, they are skills that demand ongoing cultivation, refinement, and adaptation. As information dissemination methods evolve, individuals must keep pace with changing technologies, platforms, and communication mechanisms. This lifelong learning approach ensures that individuals remain adept at navigating the nuances of the ever-changing digital landscape.

Role of Educational Institutions:

Educational institutions have a fundamental role in instilling media literacy and critical thinking skills. From early childhood education to higher education, these skills should be integrated into curricula, providing students with the tools to question, analyse, and engage with information responsibly. Teaching students to differentiate between credible sources and misinformation, critically assess arguments, and understand the impact of bias prepares them to be informed citizens.

Families as Educators:

The role of families in fostering media literacy is significant. Parents and guardians can model critical thinking, guide children in evaluating online content, and promote healthy media consumption habits. Open discussions about media, misinformation, and the power of discernment allow families to collectively build resilience against the pitfalls of uncritical consumption.

Community Engagement:

Communities also contribute to the cultivation of media literacy. Community organisations, libraries, and local events can promote workshops, discussions, and initiatives that teach individuals of all ages to navigate the digital world responsibly. Collaborative efforts within communities amplify the impact of media literacy education and create a culture of informed engagement.

Adapting to Technological Changes:

The digital landscape evolves rapidly, introducing new platforms, communication channels, and information-sharing mechanisms. Lifelong learning involves adapting to these changes and acquiring the skills to navigate emerging technologies. Understanding privacy settings, recognizing the influence of algorithms, and deciphering new forms of media are all integral aspects of media literacy in an ever-evolving digital ecosystem.

Critical Thinking as a Lifelong Skill:

Critical thinking is not confined to academic pursuits; it is a skill that enriches personal, professional, and civic life. Beyond formal education, individuals continually encounter diverse perspectives, complex issues, and persuasive arguments. The ability to question, analyse evidence, and engage in thoughtful analysis remains crucial for making informed decisions, contributing to constructive dialogues, and upholding responsible citizenship.

The Role of Fact-Checkers and Watchdogs:

We shine a spotlight on the critical role played by fact-checkers and media watchdogs in holding authorities accountable. By investigating claims, verifying information, and exposing falsehoods, these entities contribute to the maintenance of a more informed society.

In a digital landscape awash with information of varying reliability, the role of fact-checkers and media watchdogs emerges as a beacon of integrity and accountability. These entities serve as custodians of truth, wielding the power of investigation and verification to ensure that accurate information prevails over misinformation and deception. Shining a spotlight on the critical role played by fact-checkers and media watchdogs, we delve into how their efforts contribute to the maintenance of a more informed society, the fostering of critical thinking, and the holding of authorities to account.

The Fact-Checking Imperative:

Fact-checkers are dedicated to the meticulous task of verifying claims and statements made by public figures, media outlets, and various sources of information.

Armed with research, data analysis, and a commitment to transparency, fact-checkers sift through the noise to separate fact from fiction. Their goal is not only to correct misinformation but also to equip the public with accurate information to make informed decisions.

Exposing Falsehoods and Misinformation:

The impact of fact-checkers reverberates throughout society as they expose falsehoods, debunk myths, and challenge narratives that lack factual basis. By providing evidence-based corrections, fact-checkers dismantle the foundation of misinformation and help prevent its spread. Their work serves as a vital counterbalance to the rapid dissemination of unverified claims on digital platforms.

Fostering a Culture of Accountability:

Media watchdogs play a crucial role in holding authorities, institutions, and media outlets accountable for their actions and statements. These entities monitor media coverage, identify bias, analyse ethical breaches, and advocate for transparency. By shining a light on instances of bias, sensationalism, and manipulation, media watchdogs contribute to a more balanced and ethical information landscape.

Guardians of Democracy:

Fact-checkers and media watchdogs are integral to the functioning of a healthy democracy. A well-informed citizenry is essential for holding leaders accountable and making informed decisions. By providing accurate information and scrutinising those in positions of power, these entities empower citizens to engage thoughtfully in civic discourse and exercise their democratic rights.

Promoting Critical Thinking:

The work of fact-checkers and media watchdogs goes beyond correcting misinformation; it also fosters critical thinking skills. Their efforts encourage individuals to question sources, seek evidence, and evaluate claims independently. By modelling a rigorous approach to information assessment, they inspire the public to become more discerning consumers of news and information.

Navigating Challenges and Upholding Integrity:

Fact-checkers and media watchdogs face challenges, including accusations of bias, resistance from those who disseminate misinformation, and the rapid pace of digital information sharing. Upholding the integrity of their work requires transparency about their methods, commitment to nonpartisanship, and dedication to accuracy.

Bridging the Gap: The Hybrid Authority

In the midst of evolving paradigms, a new form of authority emerges – the hybrid authority. We discuss the blend of traditional expertise and new media platforms that can provide both depth of knowledge and accessibility, fostering a more inclusive information landscape.As the digital age reshapes the landscape of information sharing, a new form of authority is emerging – the hybrid authority. This dynamic entity fuses the pillars of traditional expertise with the accessibility of new media platforms, offering a unique blend of depth of knowledge and widespread reach. The rise of the hybrid authority marks a shift from rigid hierarchies to a more inclusive, adaptable, and democratised information landscape. Exploring this phenomenon, we delve into the essence of the hybrid authority, its implications for the dissemination of knowledge, and its potential to bridge the gap between established expertise and the evolving paradigms of information exchange.

Defining the Hybrid Authority:

The hybrid authority transcends the boundaries of traditional authority figures. It comprises individuals who possess expertise in their fields, often through formal education or years of experience, while also leveraging new media platforms to share their insights with a broader audience. These authorities harness the power of podcasts, social media, blogs, videos, and other digital mediums to connect directly with the public, bypassing traditional gatekeepers.

Depth of Knowledge and Accessibility:

The hybrid authority offers a unique blend of depth of knowledge and accessibility. Their expertise, honed through rigorous training and practice, provides credibility and insights that cannot be easily replicated. Simultaneously, their presence on digital platforms allows them to communicate directly with a diverse audience, breaking down geographical barriers and offering a level of accessibility that traditional authorities might struggle to achieve.

The Democratisation of Information:

The hybrid authority contributes to the democratisation of information. By leveraging digital tools, they dismantle the barriers that once limited access to expertise. This democratisation empowers individuals from various backgrounds to engage with complex subjects, fostering a more informed and diverse discourse.

Inclusivity and Evolving Paradigms:

The hybrid authority bridges the gap between traditional hierarchies and evolving paradigms of information exchange. While traditional authorities maintain their importance, the hybrid authority adapts to the changing preferences of a digital-savvy audience. This inclusivity resonates with a generation that values authenticity, engagement, and multidimensional learning experiences.

Navigating Challenges and Maintaining Integrity:

While the hybrid authority offers significant benefits, it also faces challenges. The proliferation of information on digital platforms demands that these authorities maintain rigorous standards of accuracy, transparency, and ethical conduct. Striking a balance between accessibility and credibility is a constant juggling act that requires constant vigilance.

The Future Landscape:

The emergence of hybrid authority reflects a broader shift in how we perceive expertise and authority. It highlights the need for traditional experts to adapt to digital channels, while also inspiring the next generation of experts to embrace multi-platform engagement. As digital tools continue to evolve, the hybrid authority will likely evolve with them, shaping the future landscape of information exchange.

Education for the Future: Media Literacy in Schools

We advocate for integrating media literacy education into formal curricula. By equipping students with critical thinking skills and an understanding of the digital landscape, we prepare the next generation to navigate the complexities of information and authority.In an age where information flows rapidly and the boundaries between fact and fiction blur, the need for media literacy education has never been more pressing. Integrating media literacy into formal curricula is not just a suggestion; it's a necessity. By equipping students with the tools to critically analyse information, understand the nuances of the digital landscape, and discern credible sources from misinformation, we are preparing the next generation to navigate the complexities of information, authority, and truth in a rapidly evolving world. In advocating for media literacy education, we highlight its profound significance and the transformative impact it can have on shaping responsible, informed citizens.

The Imperative of Media Literacy:

Media literacy is the ability to access, analyse, evaluate, and create media in various forms. It's about developing critical thinking skills that allow individuals to decipher the messages and intentions behind media content. In a society inundated with information from a multitude of sources, media literacy is the armour that shields students from the potential pitfalls of misinformation, manipulation, and cognitive biases.

Navigating the Digital Landscape:

The digital landscape is a double-edged sword. It offers unprecedented access to information and knowledge, but it also amplifies the spread of misinformation and biases. Media literacy education empowers students to understand how algorithms work, recognize the echo chambers created by social media, and differentiate between authentic sources and unreliable platforms.

Cultivating Critical Thinkers:

Critical thinking is the cornerstone of media literacy education. It encourages students to question assumptions, challenge narratives, and evaluate evidence. By teaching students how to approach information with scepticism, engage in fact-checking, and seek diverse perspectives, we are nurturing a generation of critical thinkers who are less likely to fall victim to manipulation or deception.

Fact-Checking and Source Evaluation:

One of the core skills of media literacy is the ability to fact-check and evaluate sources. Students learn to identify credible sources, cross-reference information, and discern whether a claim is based on evidence or conjecture. These skills extend beyond the classroom and into real-world scenarios, equipping students to make informed decisions as consumers, voters, and citizens.

Fostering Informed Citizenship:

Media literacy education goes beyond individual benefits; it contributes to the collective well-being of society. Informed citizens are better equipped to engage in civic discourse, hold authorities accountable, and participate in democratic processes. Media literacy nurtures active, responsible citizenship by encouraging students to be engaged, analytical consumers of information.

Overcoming Challenges:

Implementing media literacy education comes with challenges, such as integrating it into already packed curricula, ensuring teachers are adequately trained, and adapting to the ever-changing digital landscape. However, these challenges are outweighed by the potential rewards of a generation that is less susceptible to misinformation, more adept at navigating

complex information, and better prepared
to critically engage with the world.

Topic 3: Confirmation Bias: The Reinforcement Trap

Confirmation bias, a psychological phenomenon deeply ingrained in human cognition, wields a significant influence on how we perceive and interpret facts and authorities. Our innate tendency to seek out information that aligns with our preexisting beliefs can create a reinforcement trap, where we unwittingly reinforce our own perspectives while dismissing or ignoring conflicting evidence. In this exploration, we delve into the intricate workings of confirmation bias, dissecting its origins, manifestations, and far-reaching implications for our understanding of facts and authorities.

Origins and Evolutionary Foundations

We delve into the evolutionary roots of confirmation bias, tracing its origins to our ancestors' survival instincts. By understanding its adaptive function, we gain insights into why confirmation bias persists in the modern human psyche.Confirmation bias, a pervasive cognitive phenomenon that influences the way we perceive and process information, can trace its origins back to the evolutionary history of our species. To truly understand confirmation bias, we must delve into the ancestral contexts that shaped its emergence and appreciate its adaptive function that once contributed to our survival. By exploring its evolutionary foundations, we gain insights into why confirmation bias persists in the modern human psyche and how it can both aid and hinder our decision-making processes.

The Ancestral Landscape: Survival and Quick Decision-Making:

In the harsh environments our distant ancestors inhabited, swift decision-making was often a matter of life and death. Facing constant threats from predators, rival groups, and changing environments, our ancestors needed to process information rapidly and make decisions on the fly. Survival depended on correctly identifying cues that signalled danger or opportunity.

Confirmation Bias as a Survival Mechanism:

Confirmation bias emerged as an adaptive mechanism to enhance the efficiency of decision-making in these perilous conditions. By prioritising information that aligned with existing beliefs and expectations, our ancestors could make quicker decisions. When confronted with a potential threat, rapid recognition and avoidance based on familiar cues were more likely to result in survival than thorough evaluation.

The Drawbacks of Efficiency: Filtering Out Complexity:

While confirmation bias provided an advantage in situations where rapid response was crucial, it came with inherent limitations. The efficiency of this cognitive shortcut often meant that our ancestors filtered out complex, contradictory, or ambiguous information. This narrowing of focus could lead to a skewed perception of reality, as they primarily sought out data that confirmed their existing assumptions, beliefs, and expectations.

Confirmation Bias in the Modern World: Evolutionary Vestige and Modern Challenges:

Fast forward to the present day, and the environments our ancestors faced are vastly different from our current complex, interconnected world. Yet, the cognitive tendencies that once served as survival mechanisms continue to shape our perceptions and decision-making processes. Confirmation bias, while rooted in evolutionary advantage, can become a hindrance in situations that require open-mindedness, nuanced thinking, and accurate assessment of facts.

Mitigating the Bias: Overcoming Ancestral Instincts

Understanding the evolutionary origins of confirmation bias is the first step towards mitigating its effects. Recognizing that our minds are wired to prioritise information that aligns with our beliefs can prompt us to actively seek out diverse viewpoints, engage in critical thinking, and question our assumptions. Embracing scepticism and being open to revising our beliefs when faced with evidence can help counteract the biases that once aided our ancestors' survival.Confirmation bias, a cognitive tendency deeply rooted in our evolutionary history, can shape our perceptions and decision-making in ways that hinder our ability to objectively evaluate information. However, armed with an understanding of its origins, we possess the power to mitigate its effects and navigate the complexities of the modern world with greater intellectual clarity. By acknowledging the ancestral instincts that led to confirmation bias and embracing strategies to counteract it, we can embark on a journey of cognitive growth and open-mindedness.

Recognizing Ancestral Instincts:

To mitigate the effects of confirmation bias, it's essential to recognize that our cognitive biases have their roots in the survival mechanisms of our ancestors. Acknowledging that these biases once served a purpose in rapidly assessing threats and opportunities allows us to approach our cognitive processes with empathy and self-awareness.

Seeking Diverse Viewpoints:

One effective strategy for overcoming confirmation bias is actively seeking out diverse viewpoints. In an age of information abundance, it's crucial to expose ourselves to perspectives that challenge our existing beliefs. Engaging with differing opinions not only broadens our understanding but also fosters critical thinking skills by forcing us to evaluate and reconsider our own viewpoints.

Cultivating Critical Thinking:

Critical thinking acts as a shield against the distortion caused by confirmation bias. By consciously evaluating evidence, considering alternative explanations, and analysing the credibility of sources, we can temper the effects of biassed thinking. Cultivating critical thinking requires us to question assumptions, recognize logical fallacies, and demand evidence to support claims.

Questioning Assumptions and Beliefs:

An effective antidote to confirmation bias is the willingness to question our own assumptions and beliefs. This involves stepping back and critically examining the reasons behind our convictions. By embracing intellectual humility and recognizing that our beliefs might not be infallible, we create a mental space that allows us to entertain alternative viewpoints without feeling threatened.

Embracing Scepticism and Openness:

Scepticism is a tool for rational inquiry. Rather than accepting information at face value, a healthy dose of scepticism prompts us to scrutinise claims, verify facts, and demand well-substantiated evidence. Coupled with an openness to revising our beliefs based on new information, scepticism becomes a powerful means of countering confirmation bias.

Continuous Learning and Self-Reflection:

Mitigating confirmation bias is not a one-time endeavour; it's a lifelong commitment to continuous learning and self-reflection. Regularly reassessing our thought processes, evaluating our biases, and seeking feedback from others helps us refine our thinking and remain vigilant against the influence of confirmation bias.

The Cognitive Machinery of Confirmation Bias

Unpacking the cognitive mechanisms at play, we explore how confirmation bias operates through selective attention, interpretation, and memory. We delve into studies and experiments that reveal how this bias shapes our everyday decision-making processes.

Confirmation bias, a cognitive phenomenon that influences the way we perceive and process information, operates through a complex interplay of cognitive mechanisms. Unpacking these mechanisms reveals how our innate cognitive processes can lead us to selectively attend to, interpret, and remember information that aligns with our preexisting beliefs. By exploring the intricate workings of confirmation bias, we gain insights into its impact on everyday decision-making processes and the potential consequences for our understanding of the world.

Selective Attention: Filtering Information

At the heart of confirmation bias lies selective attention – the tendency to focus on information that confirms our existing beliefs while unconsciously ignoring or downplaying contradictory evidence. This cognitive process is a survival mechanism inherited from our ancestors who needed to quickly identify threats and opportunities in their environment. In the context of information, selective attention filters out information that challenges our worldview, leading us to consume content that reaffirms what we already know.

Interpretation and Perception: Shaping Reality

Confirmation bias extends beyond attention to the interpretation of information. When presented with ambiguous or incomplete data, our minds tend to interpret it in a way that aligns with our existing beliefs. This process can subtly distort our perception of reality, as we attribute meanings to information that reinforce our preconceptions. Even neutral information can be coloured by our biases, leading us to see what we want to see rather than what is objectively there.

Memory and Recall: Reinforcing Beliefs

Memory, another cognitive function susceptible to confirmation bias, reinforces our preexisting beliefs. We are more likely to remember information that confirms what we already think, while forgetting or misremembering information that contradicts our beliefs. This memory bias creates a feedback loop – as we recall confirming instances more readily, our convictions are further solidified, making it even harder to accept alternative viewpoints.

Studies and Experiments: Revealing the Bias in Action

Numerous studies and experiments provide insights into how confirmation bias operates in real-life scenarios. In psychology, researchers have demonstrated how participants selectively seek out and remember information that supports their opinions while ignoring opposing evidence. This bias can be observed in political contexts, where individuals tend to engage with media that aligns with their views and avoid exposure to dissenting perspectives.

Impact on Decision-Making: From Personal to Societal Consequences

Confirmation bias influences decisions both small and significant. In personal matters, it can lead to faulty judgments, reinforce stereotypes, and hinder growth. In societal contexts, it contributes to the polarisation of opinions, echo chambers in social media, and the entrenchment of misinformation. Decisions made under the influence of confirmation bias can have far-reaching consequences, impacting public policies, individual interactions, and the overall quality of discourse.Confirmation bias, a pervasive cognitive bias, exerts a profound influence on decision-making across a spectrum of contexts – from personal choices to societal dynamics. Its effects extend beyond the individual mind, shaping perceptions, interactions, and discourse at both micro and macro levels. Understanding how confirmation bias operates sheds light on its far-reaching impact, from reinforcing stereotypes to contributing to societal polarisation and misinformation.

Personal Decisions: Faulty Judgments and Hindered Growth

At a personal level, confirmation bias can lead to faulty judgments and hindered personal growth. When individuals seek out information that confirms their preexisting beliefs, they may ignore contradictory evidence that challenges their assumptions. This can lead to decisions based on incomplete or skewed information, hindering their ability to make well-informed choices. Additionally, confirmation bias can reinforce stereotypes and prevent individuals from considering alternative viewpoints, limiting their capacity for personal growth and empathy.

Societal Contexts: Polarisation, Echo Chambers, and Misinformation

In societal contexts, confirmation bias has profound implications. It contributes to the polarisation of opinions by reinforcing existing beliefs and creating a divide between different ideological camps. In the era of social media, confirmation bias is amplified by algorithmic content curation, leading to the formation of echo chambers – insulated spaces where individuals are exposed only to information that aligns with their viewpoints. This exacerbates societal divisions and impedes meaningful dialogue.

Confirmation bias also contributes to the spread of misinformation. Individuals are more likely to accept and share information that confirms their existing beliefs, even if that information is false. This perpetuates the dissemination of inaccuracies, undermining public discourse and eroding the collective pursuit of truth.

Far-Reaching Consequences: Public Policies and Quality of Discourse

Decisions made under the influence of confirmation bias can have far-reaching consequences. In the realm of public policies, confirmation bias can lead to the formulation of policies based on selective or biassed information, potentially neglecting critical perspectives and solutions. This can result in ineffective or even harmful policies that fail to address complex societal issues.

Furthermore, confirmation bias impacts the quality of public discourse. When individuals engage in discussions with a predisposition to favour information that confirms their beliefs, meaningful dialogue suffers. Constructive debates, critical engagement, and the exchange of diverse perspectives become challenging, hindering the ability to arrive at well-rounded and informed conclusions.

Mitigating the Impact: Awareness and Critical Thinking

Mitigating the impact of confirmation bias requires awareness and intentional effort. Encouraging individuals to recognize their own biases, actively seek out diverse viewpoints, and engage in critical thinking can counteract the tendency to fall into the trap of confirmation bias. By valuing evidence-based reasoning, embracing open-mindedness, and acknowledging the potential pitfalls of selective information consumption, individuals can make more well-rounded, informed decisions that contribute to a healthier discourse and a more cohesive society.

Mitigation Strategies: Navigating the Cognitive Terrain

Understanding the cognitive machinery of confirmation bias is the first step towards mitigation. By intentionally seeking out diverse viewpoints, critically evaluating evidence, and embracing open-mindedness, we can counteract its effects. Engaging in self-awareness, fact-checking, and engaging with dissenting opinions can help break the cycle of biassed thinking and contribute to more well-rounded, informed decision-making.Confirmation bias, while a natural cognitive tendency, can be mitigated through intentional efforts that foster critical thinking and open-mindedness. By understanding its mechanisms and implementing strategic approaches, individuals can navigate the cognitive terrain of confirmation bias and make more well-informed decisions that are grounded in objective analysis and a broader perspective.

1. Understanding Confirmation Bias:

Awareness is the first step toward mitigation. Understanding how confirmation bias operates – through selective attention, interpretation, and memory – enables individuals to recognize its influence on their thinking processes. Acknowledging the potential for biassed thinking encourages individuals to be more vigilant in evaluating their own beliefs and the information they encounter.

2. Seek Diverse Viewpoints:

Intentionally seek out diverse viewpoints that challenge your preexisting beliefs. Engaging with a variety of perspectives exposes you to alternative ideas and prevents the reinforcement of your own biases. This practice encourages cognitive flexibility and helps you develop a more comprehensive understanding of complex issues.

3. Evaluate Evidence Rigorously:

Develop the habit of rigorously evaluating evidence before accepting a claim. Scrutinise the quality of sources, the methodology behind studies, and the soundness of arguments. A thorough assessment of evidence can help you make decisions based on objective information rather than emotional predispositions.

4. Embrace Open-Mindedness:

Cultivate an open-minded attitude that embraces the possibility of being wrong or revising your beliefs. Approaching information with a willingness to consider different viewpoints encourages intellectual growth and prevents rigid adherence to biassed thinking patterns.

5. Engage in Self-Awareness:

Regularly reflect on your own thought processes and biases. Engage in self-examination to identify instances where you might be succumbing to confirmation bias. The practice of self-awareness allows you to catch yourself in the act of biassed thinking and encourages you to explore alternative interpretations.

6. Fact-Check and Cross-Reference:

Engage in fact-checking and cross-referencing before accepting information as true. Verify claims with reliable sources and be cautious of information that aligns too neatly with your existing beliefs. Fact-checking helps you separate factual information from misinformation or selectively presented data.

7. Engage with Dissenting Opinions:

Actively seek out and engage with dissenting opinions. Constructive debates and discussions with individuals who hold opposing views can provide new insights, challenge assumptions, and lead to a more nuanced understanding of complex issues.

8. Practice Intellectual Humility:

Cultivate intellectual humility by recognizing the limitations of your own knowledge. Accept that you may not have all the answers and be open to learning from others, even when their perspectives differ from your own.

The Reinforcement Trap: Echo Chambers and Polarisation

We examine the role of confirmation bias in the creation of echo chambers – insular environments where our existing beliefs are reinforced and opposing viewpoints are suppressed. We discuss how social media algorithms and self-selection contribute to the formation of echo chambers, fostering polarisation and hindering constructive dialogue.Confirmation bias, driven by our natural inclination to seek information that confirms our existing beliefs, can lead to a phenomenon known as the reinforcement trap. This trap manifests in the creation of echo chambers, insular environments where our viewpoints are continuously validated, and dissenting opinions are marginalised. The reinforcement trap is particularly pronounced in today's digital age, exacerbated by social media algorithms and self-selection, contributing to societal polarisation and undermining the potential for meaningful dialogue.

Echo Chambers: The Self-Perpetuating Cycle of Confirmation

Echo chambers are virtual bubbles where individuals are exposed to information and perspectives that align with their preexisting beliefs. Inside these chambers, confirmation bias thrives, as individuals are surrounded by content that constantly reinforces what they already think. This self-perpetuating cycle solidifies their views and discourages engagement with diverse viewpoints.

Social Media Algorithms: Amplifying Confirmation Bias

Social media platforms, designed to maximise engagement and retention, often employ algorithms that curate content based on users' past interactions and preferences. While these algorithms aim to provide personalised content, they inadvertently amplify confirmation bias. They show users content similar to what they've engaged with before, which creates a feedback loop of reinforcing information. Users are exposed to content that resonates with their beliefs, and dissenting perspectives become less visible.

Self-Selection and Content Consumption: Reinforcing Biases

Individuals also contribute to the formation of echo chambers through self-selection. People tend to follow or connect with others who share similar views, and they consume media that aligns with their beliefs. This self-selection limits exposure to diverse perspectives and fosters an environment where confirmation bias flourishes. People are more likely to unfollow or ignore those who challenge their beliefs, further deepening the echo chamber effect.

Polarisation: A Consequence of Echo Chambers

The formation of echo chambers nurtures polarisation – the increasing divide between differing ideological groups. As individuals are exposed primarily to information that supports their existing beliefs, they become more entrenched in their positions. This polarisation not only inhibits empathy and understanding but also leads to more extreme viewpoints and less willingness to engage in constructive dialogue.

Hindrance to Constructive Dialogue:

Echo chambers hinder the potential for meaningful and informed discussions. In an environment where conflicting viewpoints are suppressed, the exchange of diverse ideas becomes rare. Constructive dialogue requires exposure to diverse perspectives, critical analysis, and the willingness to consider alternative viewpoints. Echo chambers stifle these essential components of productive discourse.

Breaking the Reinforcement Trap:

Breaking free from the reinforcement trap requires conscious effort. Individuals can intentionally seek out diverse sources of information, engage with content that challenges their beliefs, and participate in discussions with those who hold differing views. Media literacy education plays a pivotal role in teaching individuals to recognize echo chambers and actively counteract confirmation bias.

Case Studies: Confirmation Bias in Action:
 Biases:

We discuss strategies for cultivating intellectual humility – the antidote to the illusion of control and overconfidence. By embracing uncertainty, valuing diverse perspectives, and fostering a growth mindset, readers can navigate the biases that cloud their perception of facts and authorities.In order to understand the profound impact of confirmation bias, examining real-life case studies is essential. These case studies illustrate how confirmation bias can distort perceptions, reinforce existing beliefs, and hinder the quest for accurate information. Alongside these examples, strategies for cultivating intellectual humility – a critical mindset to counteract biases – can be explored. Intellectual humility serves as the antidote to the illusion of control and overconfidence, enabling individuals to approach information with a balanced, open-minded perspective.

Case Study 1: Political Echo Chambers on Social Media

In the realm of social media, confirmation bias can lead to the formation of political echo chambers. Users tend to follow or engage with content that aligns with their political beliefs. As a result, their feeds become saturated with information that reinforces their existing views, while dissenting perspectives are pushed to the periphery. This insular environment can lead to heightened polarisation, where individuals become more entrenched in their positions, inhibiting meaningful dialogue across the political spectrum.

Case Study 2: Medical Misinformation and Vaccine Hesitancy

Confirmation bias plays a significant role in the spread of medical misinformation and vaccine hesitancy. When individuals hold deep-seated beliefs about the risks of vaccines, they are more likely to seek out and trust information that confirms their fears. This can lead to the rejection of scientific evidence supporting the safety and efficacy of vaccines. The confirmation bias-driven echo chambers within certain communities contribute to the persistence of harmful misinformation, affecting public health efforts.

Strategies for Cultivating Intellectual Humility:

1. Embrace Uncertainty:

Recognize that your understanding of complex issues may be limited and subject to change. Intellectual humility involves acknowledging that there is always more to learn and that your current perspective might be incomplete.

2. Value Diverse Perspectives:

Actively seek out and engage with viewpoints that challenge your beliefs. Engaging with diverse perspectives fosters empathy, broadens your understanding, and helps you recognize the limitations of your own viewpoints.

3. Foster a Growth Mindset:

Adopt a growth mindset that embraces learning and development. Understand that mistakes and changes in perspective are a natural part of intellectual growth, rather than signs of weakness.

4. Practise Active Listening:

When engaging in discussions, practise active listening by genuinely considering others' viewpoints before formulating a response. This approach fosters deeper understanding and encourages open-mindedness.

5. Seek Feedback:

Welcome constructive feedback from others. Accepting criticism and being open to different interpretations of situations can enhance your ability to view issues from multiple angles.

6. Engage in Self-Reflection:

Regularly reflect on your own thought processes and decisions. Consider whether your biases are influencing your thinking and explore ways to counteract their effects.

Media Literacy and Overcoming Overconfidence

In the digital age, media literacy becomes a critical tool for countering the impact of overconfidence bias. We explore how recognizing our cognitive limitations and developing critical thinking skills can empower individuals to engage with authorities and information sources more effectively.

In the digital age, where information is abundant and easily accessible, overconfidence bias can lead individuals to overestimate their understanding and make decisions based on incomplete or biassed information. Media literacy emerges as a crucial tool to counteract the impact of overconfidence bias, allowing individuals to navigate the complex digital landscape with greater discernment and critical thinking. By recognizing cognitive limitations and developing media literacy skills, individuals can engage with authorities and information sources more effectively.

Overconfidence Bias in the Digital Age:

Overconfidence bias is the tendency to believe that our judgments and decisions are more accurate than they actually are. In the context of the digital age, this bias can manifest as individuals assuming they possess comprehensive knowledge based on cursory exposure to information online. This can lead to hasty judgments, misguided beliefs, and a disregard for diverse perspectives.

The Role of Media Literacy:

Media literacy equips individuals with the skills to evaluate, analyse, and interpret information critically. It goes beyond recognizing reliable sources; it involves understanding the nuances of bias, the impact of media manipulation, and the techniques used to convey information persuasively. By cultivating media literacy, individuals develop the ability to question, verify, and engage with information in a more informed manner.

Recognizing Cognitive Limitations:

Media literacy prompts individuals to recognize their cognitive limitations and the potential for overconfidence bias. It encourages humility in the face of complex issues and an understanding that comprehensive understanding often requires diligent research, critical analysis, and engagement with diverse perspectives.

Developing Critical Thinking Skills:

Media literacy fosters the development of critical thinking skills, which are vital for overcoming overconfidence bias. Critical thinking encourages individuals to question assumptions, evaluate evidence, and consider alternative viewpoints before forming conclusions. This practice helps individuals approach information with a healthy dose of scepticism and a willingness to engage in deeper analysis.

Engaging Effectively with Authorities:

Media literacy enables individuals to engage more effectively with authorities and information sources. Rather than accepting information uncritically, individuals learn to assess the credibility of sources, evaluate the methodology behind claims, and discern between factual reporting and opinion. By applying critical thinking skills, individuals can engage with authorities in a manner that is intellectually rigorous and well-informed.

www.ingramcontent.com/pod-product-compliance
Lightning Source LLC
Chambersburg PA
CBHW071605270726
48661CB00018B/1250